Intermediate to Advanced Piano Solo

THE WORLD'S GREAT CLASSICAL MUSIC

Tchaikovsky

47 Selections from Symphonies, Concertos, Operas, Ballets and Piano Works

EDITED BY BLAKE NEELY AND RICHARD WALTERS

Cover Painting: Kandinsky, *Odessa–Port I*, 1898

ISBN 978-0-634-01637-0

7777 W. BLUEMOUND RD. P.O. BOX 13819 MILWAUKEE, WI 53213

Visit Hal Leonard Online at
www.halleonard.com

CONTENTS

*Pieces originally for piano; the remaining works are piano transcriptions.

Had Russian composer Pyotr Il'yich Tchaikovsky (1840–1893) honored his family's wishes, he would have become a lawyer. When he was ten years old, about the same time he began to compose, his family enrolled him in the School of Jurisprudence in St. Petersburg. He trained for a career in law and worked as a clerk in the Russian Ministry of Justice for about five years before mustering the courage to defy his family and study music. Tchaikovsky was 23 when he finally entered the St. Petersburg Conservatory, where he studied with Anton Rubinstein. At 25 he was appointed professor of composition at the newly founded Conservatory of Music in Moscow.

Although the composer who gave us *Swan Lake*, the *Symphony Pathétique* and *The Nutcracker* clearly had the creative abilities to support his musical ambitions, his personality was not well suited to the public life this career brought him. Tchaikovsky was from childhood painfully shy and overly sensitive to any form of criticism or perceived slight. He had a delicate, nervous nature and suffered from bouts of absolute self-loathing. In the early years of his musical career his self-critical view led him to destroy many of his own scores. His personal sufferings were exacerbated by being homosexual in a society that placed severe legal penalties and strict social taboos on that orientation.

In the early years of his career, Tchaikovsky's musical interests were strikingly diverse. During those years he wrote the opera *The Oprichnik*, the *Romeo and Juliet Fantasy-Overture*, his first two symphonies, as well as a set of sentimental songs and a string quartet. (By an unlikely turn of events a refrain from the quartet's slow movement made it to America's Tin Pan Alley as the song "The Isle of May.") He also had an interest in writing which led him to work as a music critic for four years. In 1875 Tchaikovsky began to work on an important ballet, calling it *Swan Lake*, That same year he produced his *Piano Concerto No. 1*, dedicated to Nikolay Rubinstein, who declared it unplayable and rejected the honor of the dedication. Deeply wounded by this, Tchaikovsky rededicated the piece to Hans von Bülow, who performed the world premiere in Boston.

In 1877 Tchaikovsky began two very different but equally strange relationships with two women. Nadezhda Filaretovna von Meck was a wealthy widow who was perhaps as shy as Tchaikovsky. The two began a correspondence that would continue for 14 years. In 1878 she became Tchaikovsky's benefactress, providing him with an income that allowed him to resign his teaching post and devote his energies to composing. The pair agreed at the outset of their relationship that they would never meet, though through their intimate letters they bared their souls to one another. On two separate occasions, when they chanced to pass one another on the street, they each hurried away without stopping to say hello.

The other woman in Tchaikovsky's life at this time was Antonina Milyukova, his wife. They met after Antonina, who was enamored of Tchaikovsky, threatened to commit suicide if he would not agree to see her. Tchaikovsky entered the marriage for the sake of appearances, making it clear that this was to be a marriage in name only. Once they were married, Antonina decided the arrangement was not suitable and began making demands on the composer that he could not fulfill. He fled to his sister's country home, but his schedule eventually demanded that he return to Moscow. When the situation with his wife worsened Tchaikovsky attempted suicide by throwing himself into the Moscow River. He was sent to Switzerland to recover, with doctor's instructions that he was not to return to his wife. Theirs was a messy divorce, complete with Antonina attempting to humiliate Tchaikovsky via letters to his family, friends and publisher. Tchaikovsky hired a private detective to investigate Antonina's desperate actions.

During 1887, Tchaikovsky spent several weeks at the bedside of his dear friend Nikolay Kondryatin, as Kondryatin died a slow death from syphilis, or perhaps from the "cure" of high doses of mercury. Soon afterwards, grieving the loss of his friend, he began work on the *Fifth Symphony*, writing such notes on the piece as "Introduction: complete submission before fate...", and "Allegro: murmur of doubt, complaints, reproaches... No, no hope."

Although most people remember Tchaikovsky for his ballets and symphonies, it was opera that really captured his interest. His interest in opera began when he was still in his teens, long before he had the ability to compose such an involved work. Tchaikovsky's first opera, *The Voyevoda*, premiered in 1869, when the composer was 29 years old. It had a five performance run, after which Tchaikovsky destroyed the score. Parts of the opera were reworked in the later opera *The Oprichnik*. His second opera, *Undina*, never made it to the stage. *The Oprichnik* premiered in St. Petersburg in 1874, but in the end Tchaikovsky was displeased with this work as well. *Vakula the Smith* premiered in 1876, followed by *Cherevichka* in 1887, and his most popular opera, *Eugene Onegin*, in 1879. *The Maid of Orleans*, an opera about Joan of Arc, opened in 1881, followed by *Mazeppa* in 1884, *The Sorceress* in 1887 and *The Queen of Spades* in 1890. Tchaikovsky's operas mirror the various stages in his musical life, from the strong nationalism in his earlier works to a progressive, more eclectic style in his later years.

Tchaikovsky's last opera, *Iolanthe*, was first heard in December of 1892. It was immediately eclipsed by the two act work with which it was paired, *The Nutcracker*. While the composer was working on the two pieces, it was *Iolanthe* that occupied his attention. *The Nutcracker* was written in a hurry, on a commission, to a plot that lacked dramatic cohesiveness or momentum. Rimsky-Korsakov criticized the ballet, saying it was "completely devoid of creativity." But the public loved it. It has become a holiday classic, playing throughout the world every year. It is clearly the music to *The Nutcracker* that has given it its enduring appeal. The first time excerpts of music were heard, in an Imperial Music Society preliminary performance, five of the selections had to be repeated to answer vigorous applause.

In 1890 Tchaikovsky's long, curious relationship with Nadezhda von Meck came to an end. His sister died that same year. Despite these personal losses, his musical endeavors were increasingly successful. In 1891 he visited America and conducted at the opening of Carnegie Hall in New York City. In 1893 he completed his *Sixth Symphony*, the *Pathétique*, and traveled to England to receive an honorary degree from Cambridge.

That same year, during a cholera epidemic in Russia, Tchaikovsky knowingly drank unboiled water while dining with his brother Modest. Modest reported that his brother claimed to have no fear of the disease. According to Modest, Tchaikovsky was struck ill with cholera and died a few days later, just nine days after the premiere of the *Pathétique*. It was Tchaikovsky's wish that the world remember his music rather than the sometimes embarrassing details of his personal life. Modest did his part to fulfill that wish, writing a three-volume biography that cast his brother in a positive light. The biography stood for many years as the definitive work on the composer. But from the moment Tchaikovsky's death was announced, rumors of his having committed suicide swirled about Moscow. The rumors had enough weight that even *Grove's Dictionary of Music and Musicians* mentioned the rumors in an edition published just a few years later.

One rumor speculated that the suicide was over the poor reception of the *Pathétique*. Another suggested that the suicide was ordered by the Czar, following Tchaikovsky's romantic encounters with members of his court. In 1980 a Russian musicologist who had emigrated to the U.S. claimed to have discovered that Tchaikovsky had been instructed to take arsenic by his law school classmates, who were worried that the composer's homosexual lifestyle would cast a pall on their school's reputation. Whatever the case, by the time of his death, the 54 year old composer looked much older than his years. Personal struggles and losses had taken a terrible toll on the fragile man.

— Elaine Schmidt

Andante cantabile
from STRING QUARTET, OP. 11

Pyotr Il'yich Tchaikovsky
1840–1893
originally for string quartet

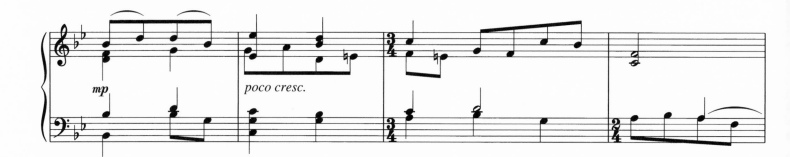

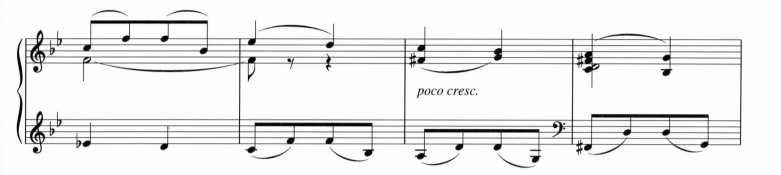

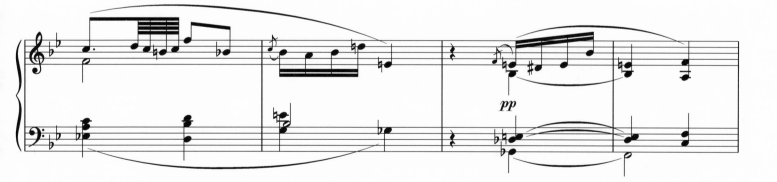

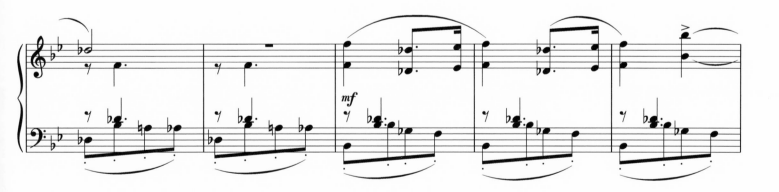

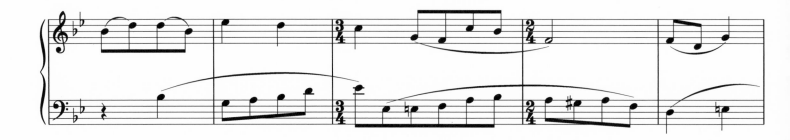

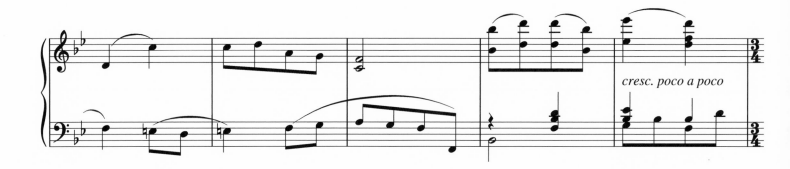

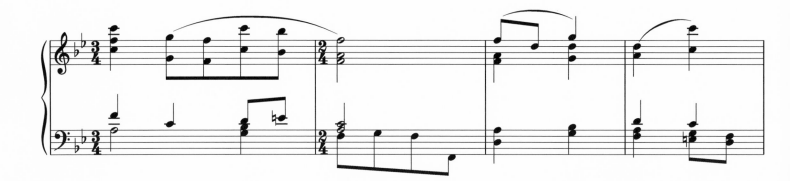

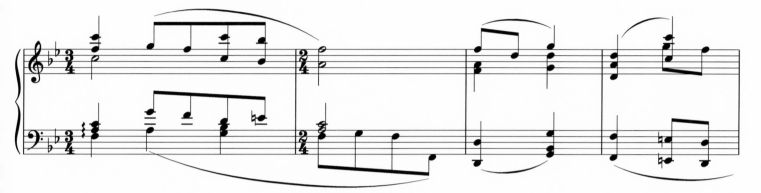

12

La melodia molto espressiva ed un poco marcato,
l'accompagnamento sempre **ppp**

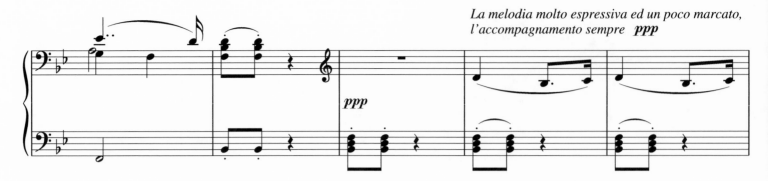

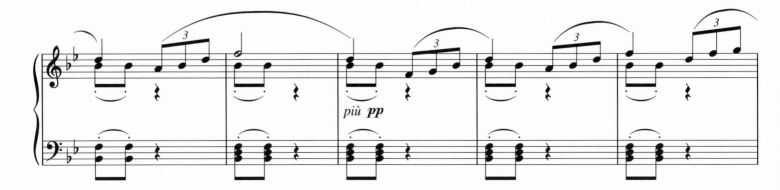

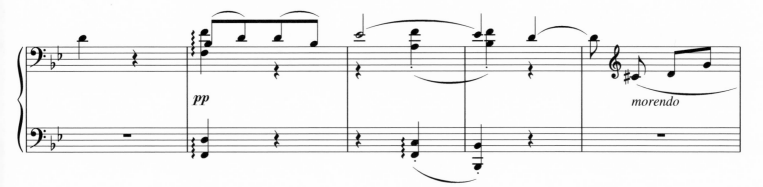

Barcarolle in G Minor (June)
from THE SEASONS

Pyotr Il'yich Tchaikovsky
1840–1893
Op. 37, No. 6

Andante cantabile

Poco più mosso

Allegro giocoso

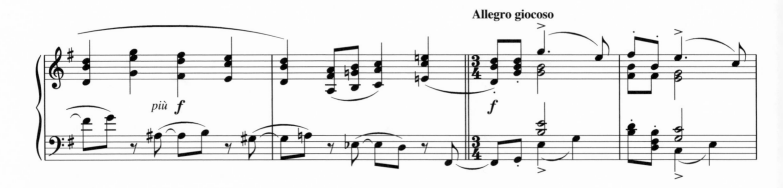

8va

Tempo I

Andante cantabile

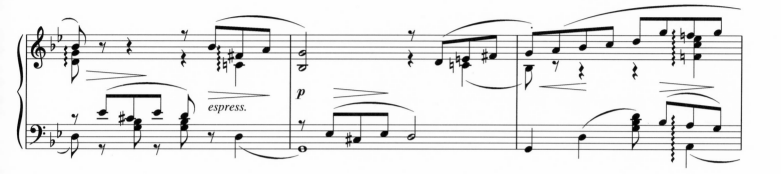

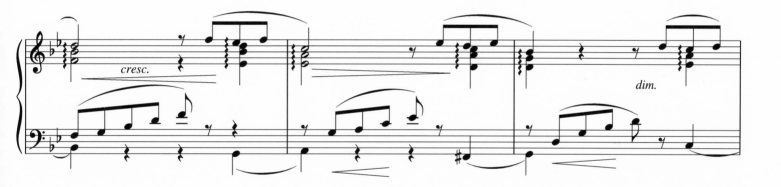

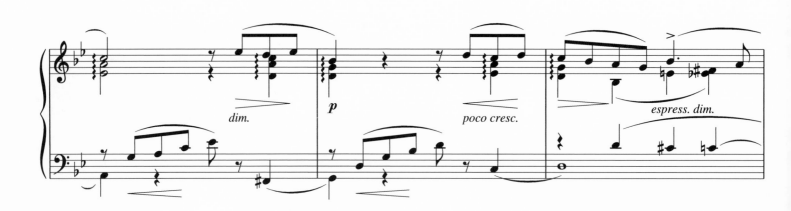

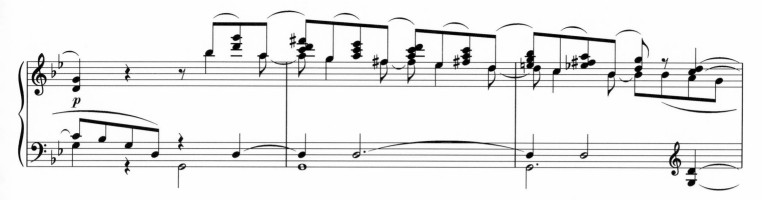

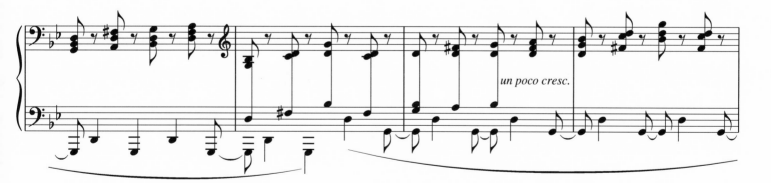

Capriccio Italien
Opening Theme

Pyotr Il'yich Tchaikovsky
1840-1893
Op. 45
originally for orchestra

Andante un poco rubato

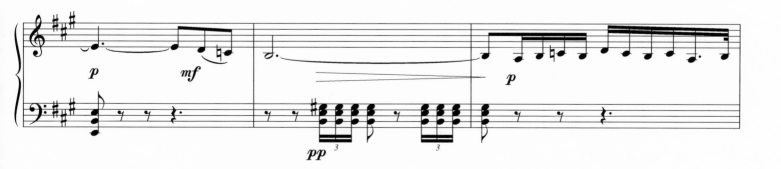

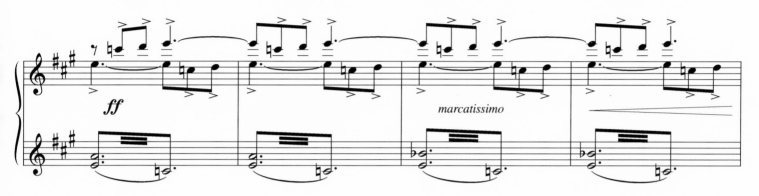

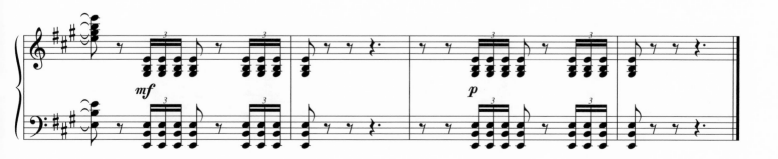

1812 Overture
Excerpt

Pyotr Il'yich Tchaikovsky
1840-1893
Op. 49
originally for orchestra

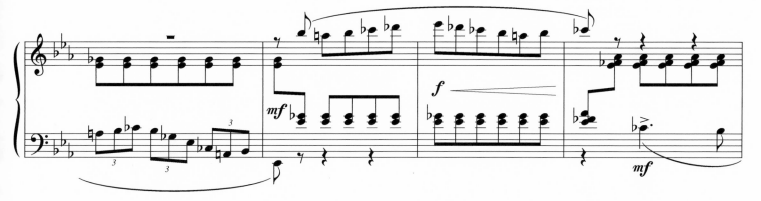

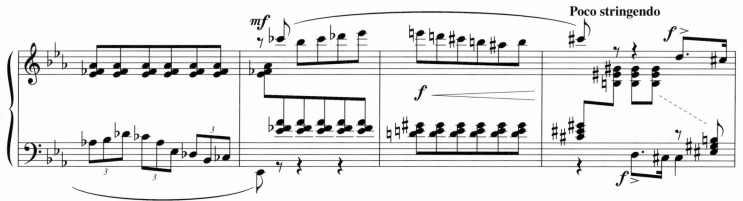

Poco stringendo

Poco più mosso

cresc.

Allegro giusto (♩ = 138)

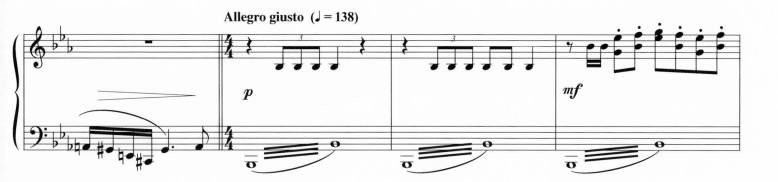

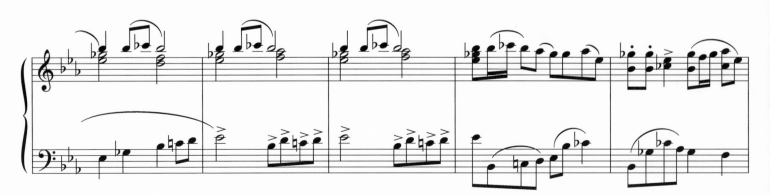

Allegro vivace

sempre ff

marcato

ff

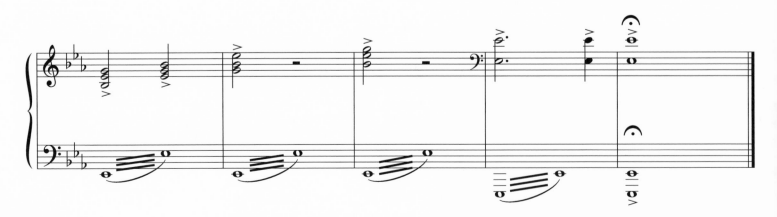

Chanson napolitaine

from ALBUM POUR ENFANTS

Pyotr Il'yich Tchaikovsky
1840-1893
Op. 39, No. 18

Moderato (♩ = 92)

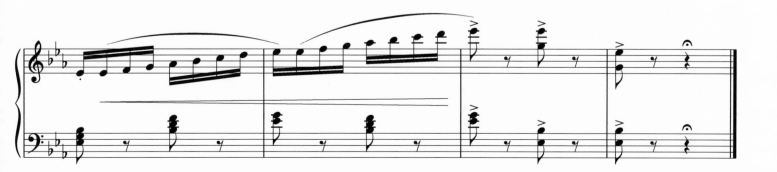

Chant sans paroles

from SOUVENIR DE HAPSAL

Pyotr Il'yich Tchaikovsky
1840–1893
Op. 2, No. 3

Allegretto grazioso e cantabile

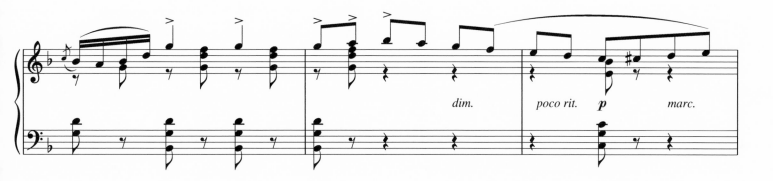

Tempo I

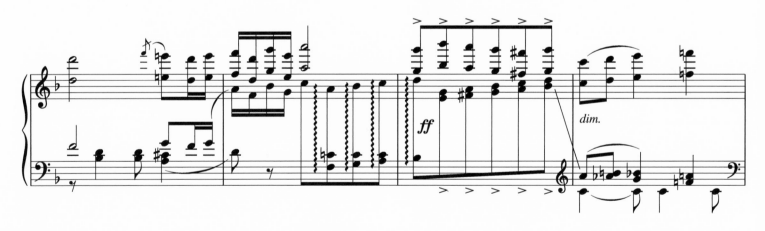

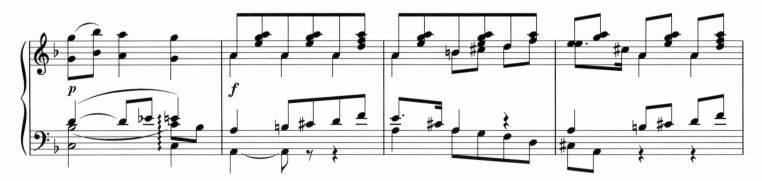

35

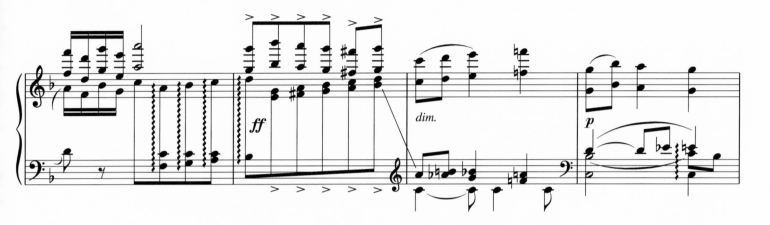

sempre diminuendo

marcato la melodia

Chanson triste
from DOUZE MORCEAUX

Pyotr Il'yich Tchaikovsky
1840-1893
Op. 40, No. 2

Allegro non troppo
la melodia con molta espressione

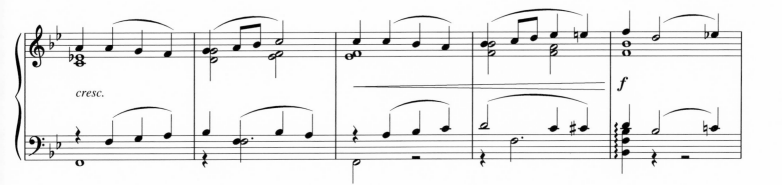

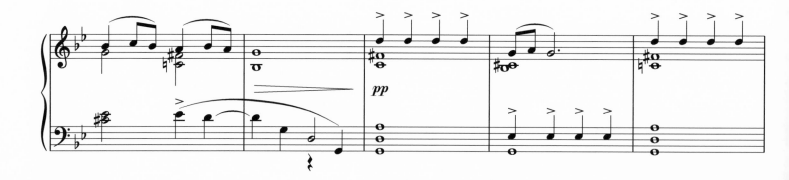

Lenski's Aria
from the opera EUGENE ONEGIN

Pyotr Il'yich Tchaikovsky
1840-1893
originally for tenor and orchestra

Andante

Poco più animato

Andante mosso

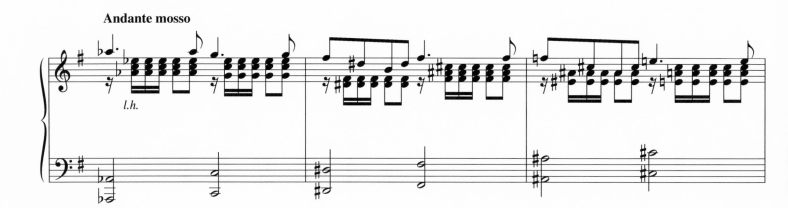

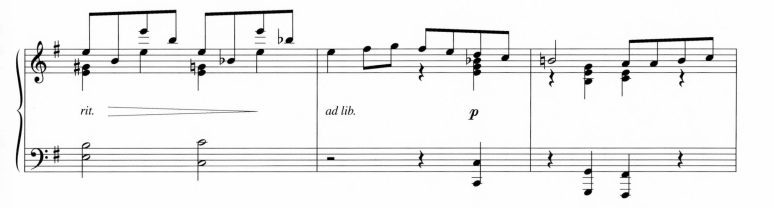

Polonaise
from the opera EUGENE ONEGIN
Excerpt

Pyotr Il'yich Tchaikovsky
1840-1893
originally for orchestra

Allegro moderato (♩ = 104)

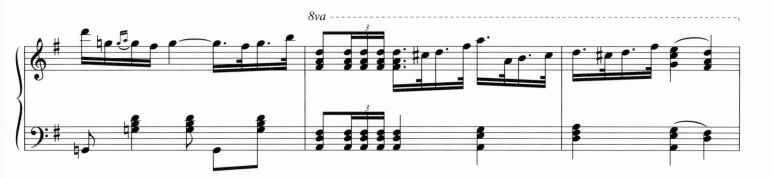

Waltz
from the opera EUGENE ONEGIN

Pyotr Il'yich Tchaikovsky
1840–1893
originally for orchestra and chorus

Tempo di Valse (Entr'acte Waltz)

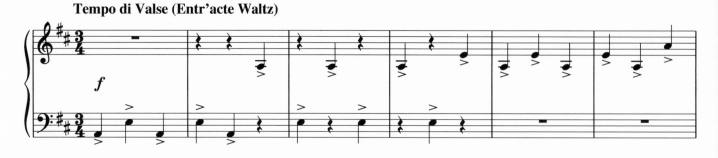

Mazurka de Salon
from TROIS MORCEAUX

Pyotr Il'yich Tchaikovsky
1840–1893
Op. 9, No. 3

[Moderately]

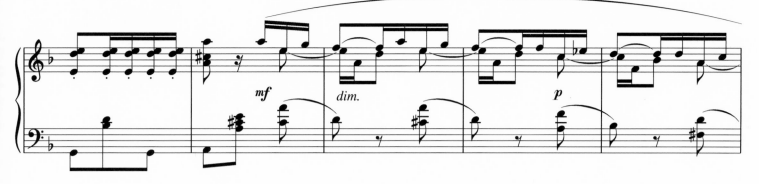

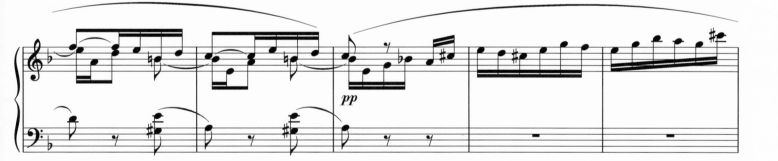

marcato il canto

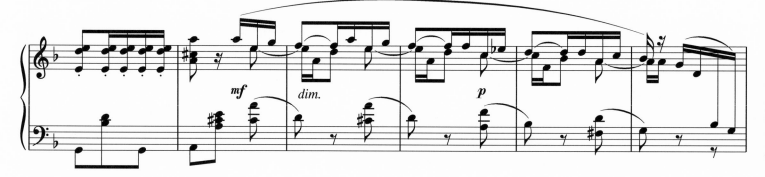

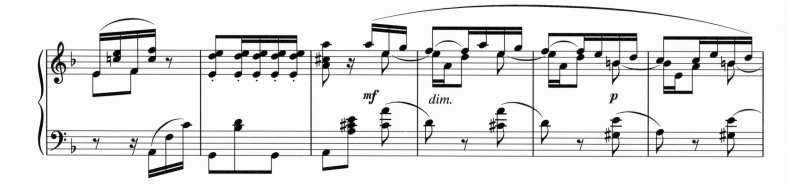

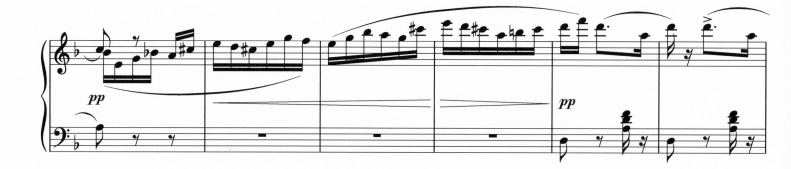

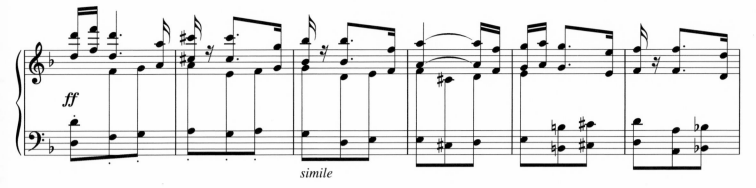

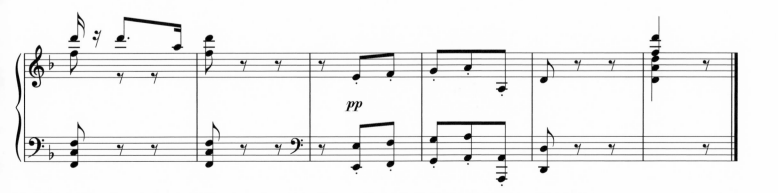

Mélodie
from SOUVENIR D'UN LIEU CHER

Pyotr Il'yich Tchaikovsky
1840–1893
Op. 42, No. 3
originally for violin and piano

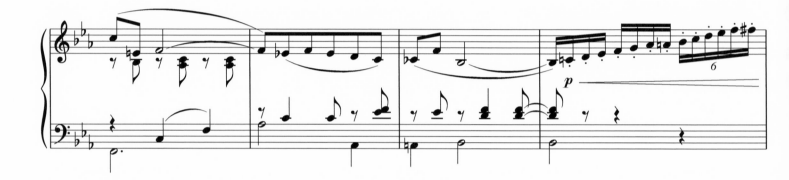

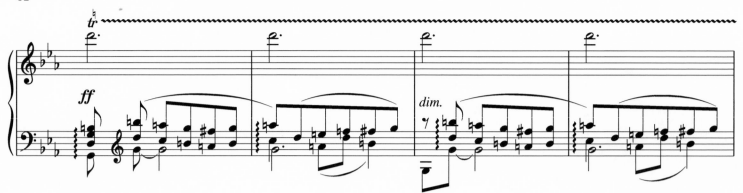

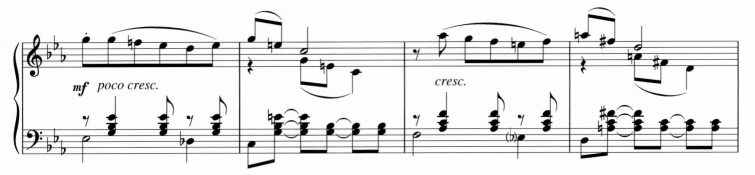

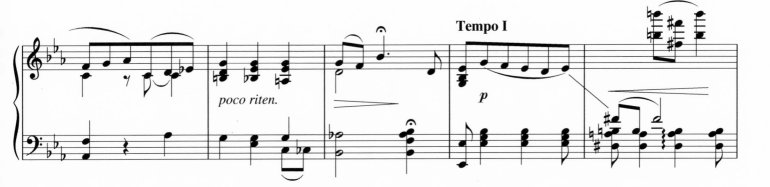

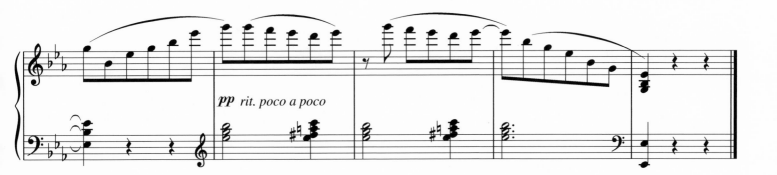

Marche Slav

Themes

Pyotr Il'yich Tchaikovsky
1840-1893
Op. 31
originally for orchestra

Grave quasi marcia funebre

Original key: B-flat minor.

L'istesso tempo

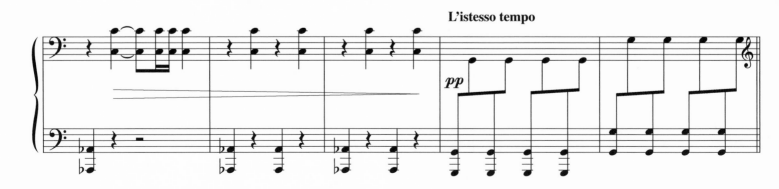

Andante maestoso

Allegro risoluto vivace

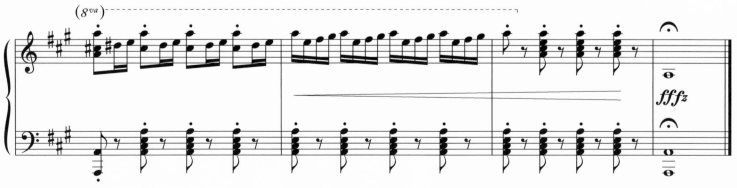

Nocturne

Pyotr Il'yich Tchaikovsky
1840–1893
Op. 10, No. 1

Andante cantabile

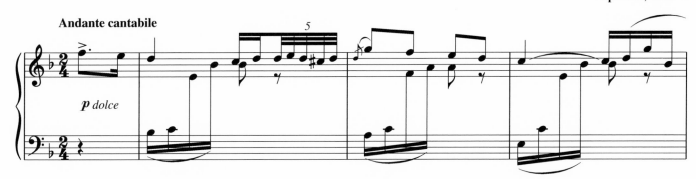

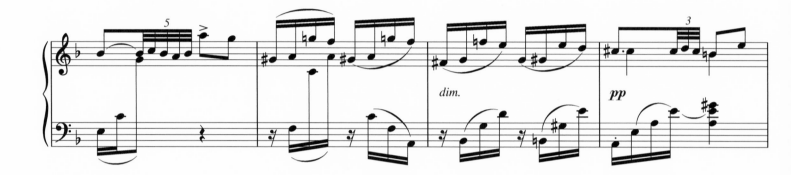

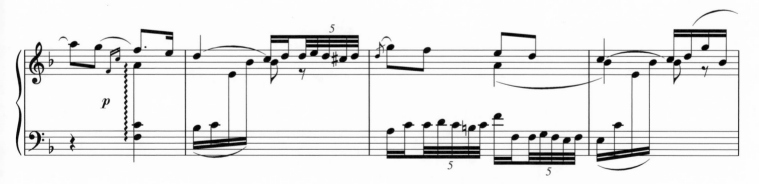

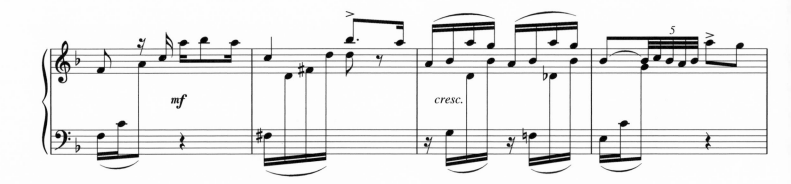

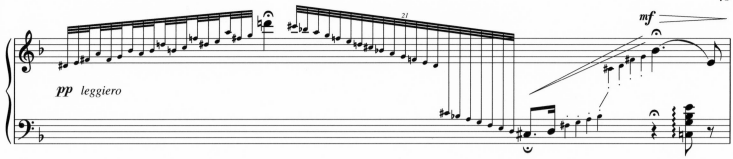

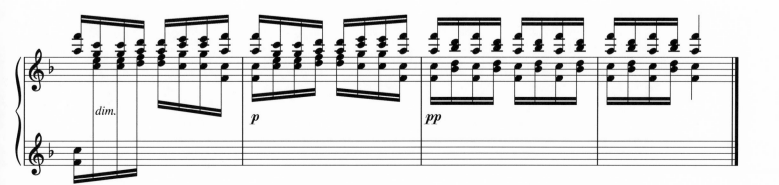

Nur wer die Sehnsucht kennt
(None but the lonely heart)

Pyotr Il'yich Tchaikovsky
1840-1893
Op. 6
originally for voice and piano

Andante non tanto

Arabian Dance
("Coffee")
from the ballet THE NUTCRACKER

Pyotr Il'yich Tchaikovsky
1840-1893
Op. 71
originally for orchestra

Allegretto

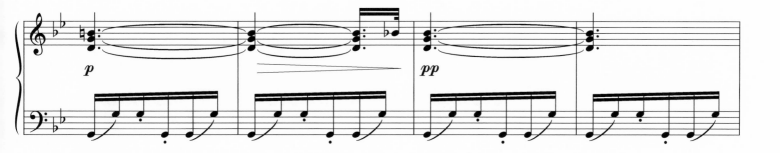

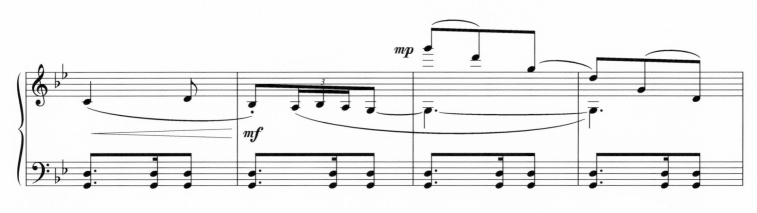

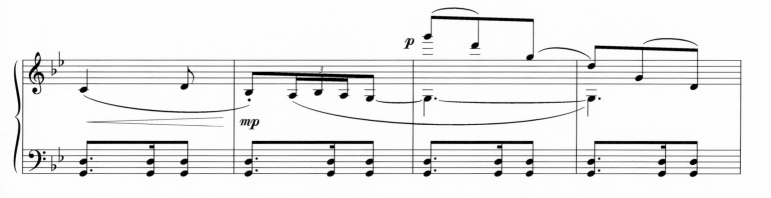

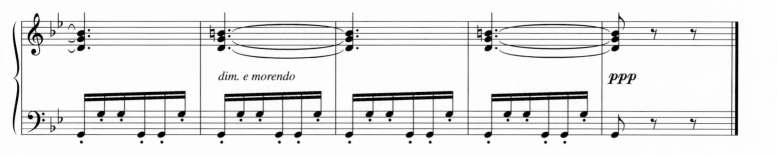

Chinese Dance
("Tea")
from the ballet THE NUTCRACKER

Pyotr Il'yich Tchaikovsky
1840-1893
Op. 71
originally for orchestra

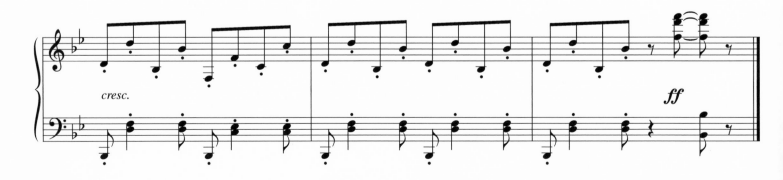

Russian Dance
(Trépak)
from the ballet THE NUTCRACKER

Pyotr Il'yich Tchaikovsky
1840-1893
Op. 71
originally for orchestra

Tempo di trépak, molto vivace

Dance of the Reed-Flutes

from the ballet THE NUTCRACKER

Pyotr Il'yich Tchaikovsky
1840–1893
Op. 71
originally for orchestra

Dance of the Sugar Plum Fairy

from the ballet THE NUTCRACKER

Pyotr Il'yich Tchaikovsky
1840–1893
Op. 71
originally for orchestra

Andante ma non troppo

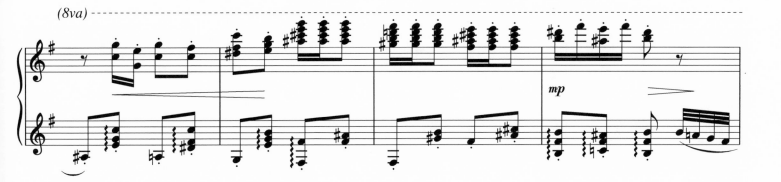

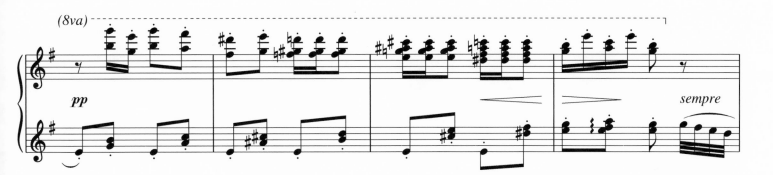

Waltz of the Flowers
from the ballet THE NUTCRACKER
Excerpt

Pyotr Il'yich Tchaikovsky
1840-1893
Op. 71
originally for orchestra

Tempo di valse

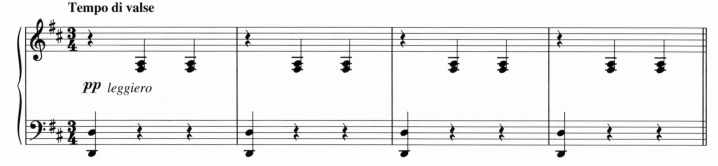

dolce cantando

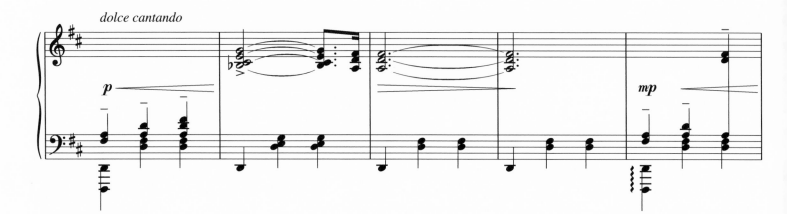

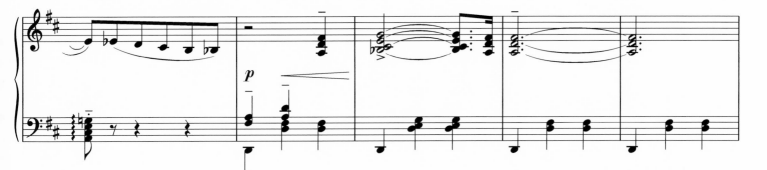

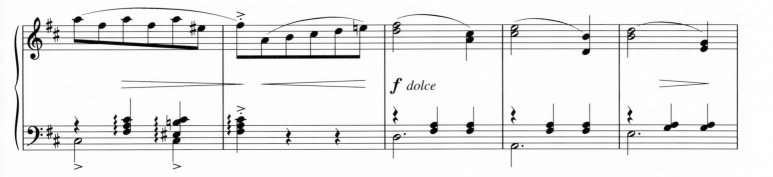

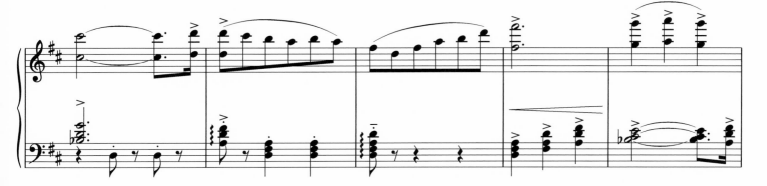

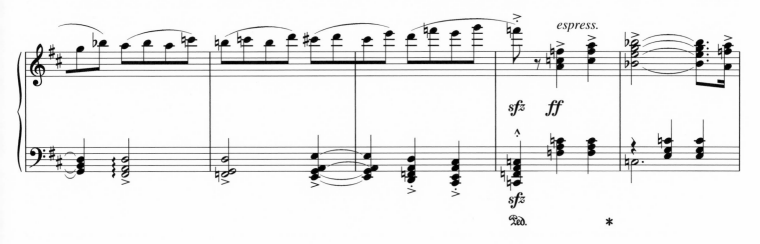

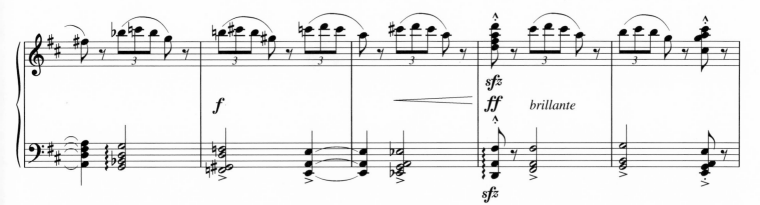

Piano Concerto No. 1 in B-flat Minor
First Movement Excerpt

Pyotr Il'yich Tchaikovsky
1840-1893
Op. 23
originally for piano and orchestra

Andante maestoso

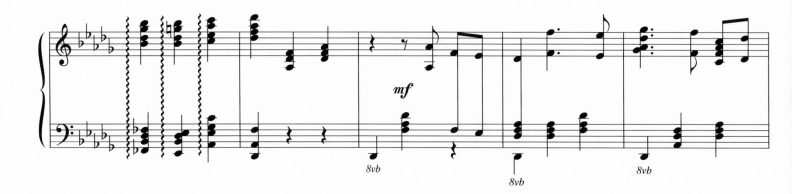

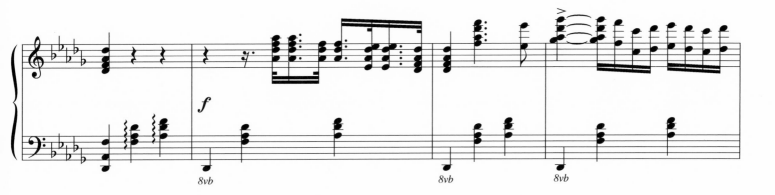

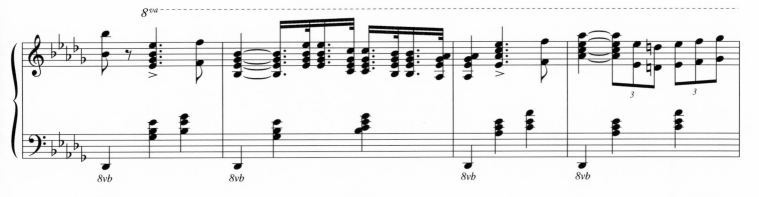

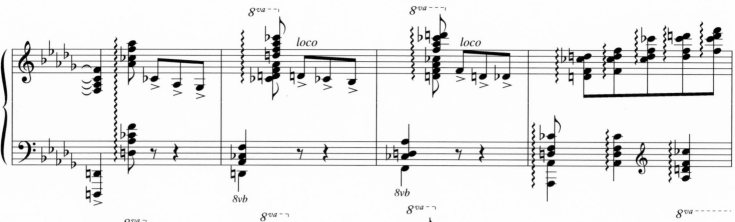

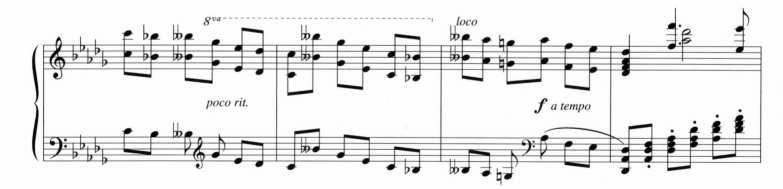

Piano Concerto No. 1 in B-flat Minor
Second Movement Excerpt

Pyotr Il'yich Tchaikovsky
1840-1893
Op. 23
originally for piano and orchestra

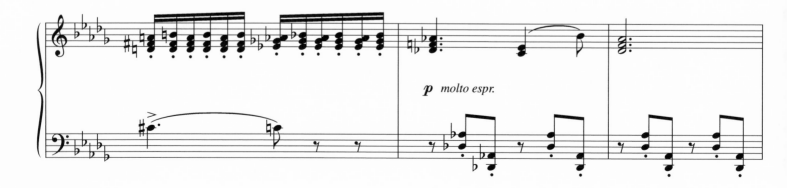

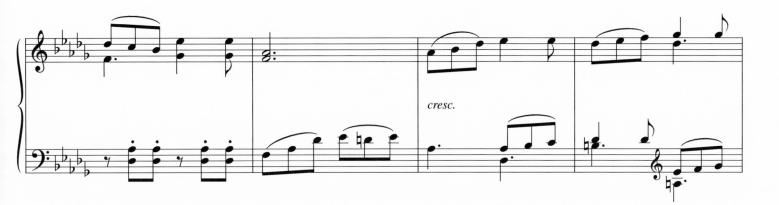

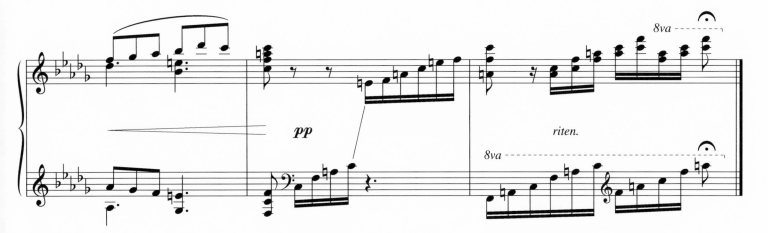

Piano Concerto No. 1 in B-flat Minor

Third Movement Excerpt

Pyotr Il'yich Tchaikovsky
1840-1893
Op. 23
originally for piano and orchestra

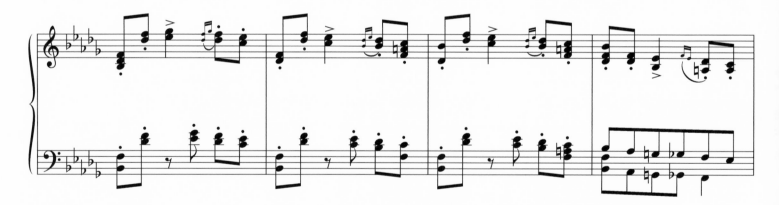

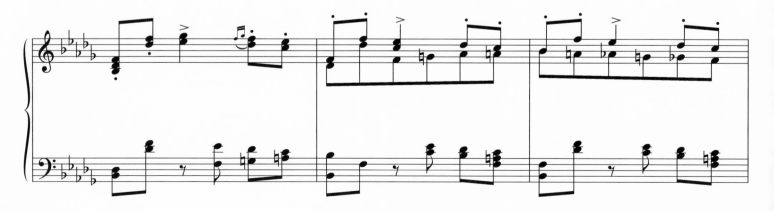

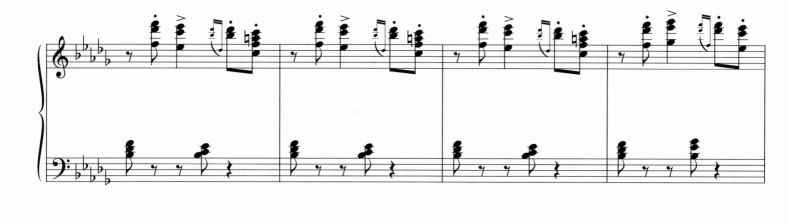

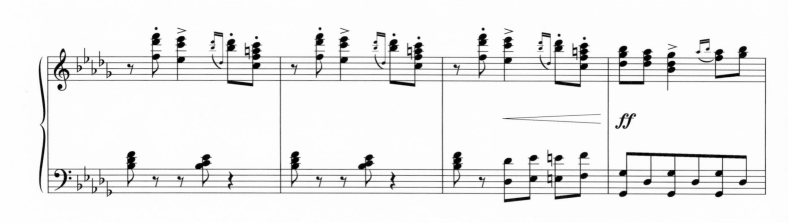

Piano Concerto No. 2 in G Major

First Movement Excerpt

Pyotr Il'yich Tchaikovsky
1840-1893
Op. 44
originally for piano and orchestra

Allegro brillante e molto vivace

Piano Concerto No. 2 in G Major
Third Movement Excerpt

Pyotr Il'yich Tchaikovsky
1840-1893
Op. 44
originally for piano and orchestra

Polka de Salon

from TROIS MORCEAUX

Pyotr Il'yich Tchaikovsky
1840–1893
Op. 9, No. 2

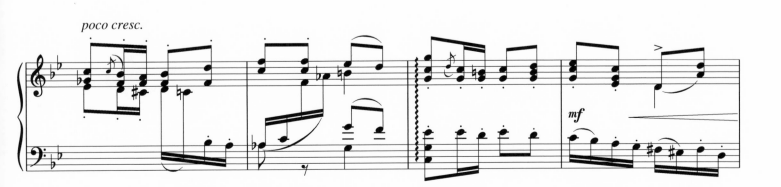

The Queen of Spades

(Pique Dame)
Introduction from the opera

Pyotr Il'yich Tchaikovsky
1840-1893
Op. 68
originally for orchestra

Andante mosso (♩. = 84)

poco dim.

mf

p

>

pp

Rêverie du soir
from SIX MORCEAUX

Pyotr Il'yich Tchaikovsky
1840–1893
Op. 19, No. 1

Andanted espressivo

L'istesso tempo

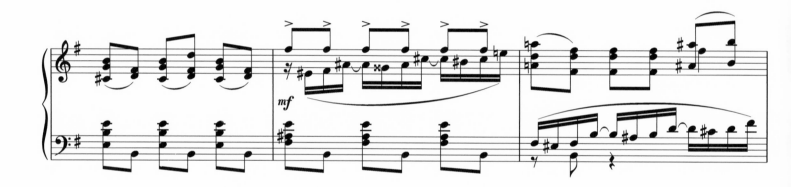

Romance

Pyotr Il'yich Tchaikovsky
1840-1893
Op. 5

Andante cantabile

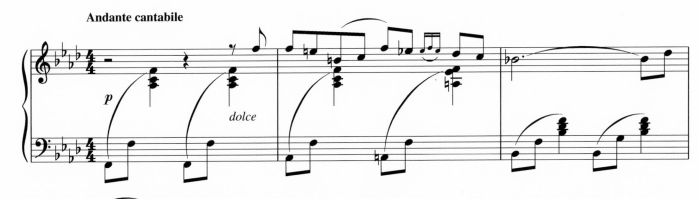

poco a poco accel.

cresc.

Allegro energico

mf

f

ff

Tempo I

molto più mosso *dimin.*

Allegro

ritard.

Romeo and Juliet

Fantasy Overture
Love Theme

Pyotr Il'yich Tchaikovsky
1840-1893
originally for orchestra

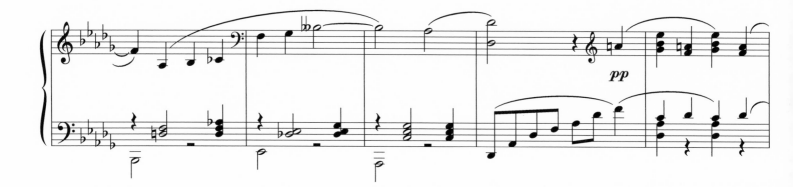

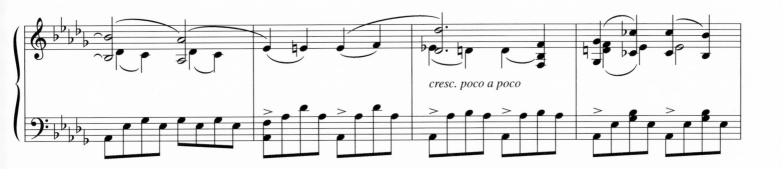

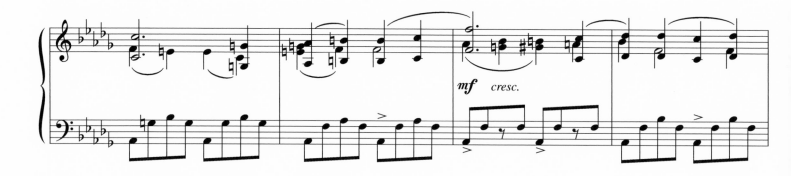

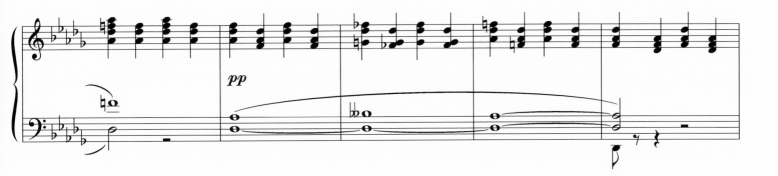

Serenade in C
First Movement Excerpt

Pyotr Il'yich Tchaikovsky
1840-1893
Op. 48
originally for strings

Andante non troppo (♩. = 72)

Allegro moderato (♩. = 84)

cresc.　　　mf　　　　　　　　　　　ff

f

Serenade in C
Second Movement Excerpt
("Waltz")

Pyotr Il'yich Tchaikovsky
1840-1893
Op. 48
originally for strings

Moderato, Tempo di Valse

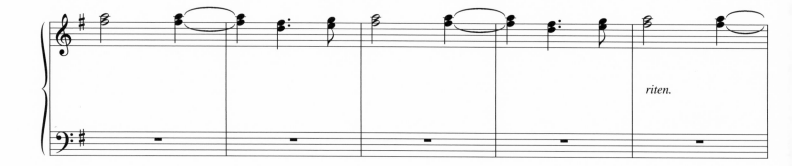

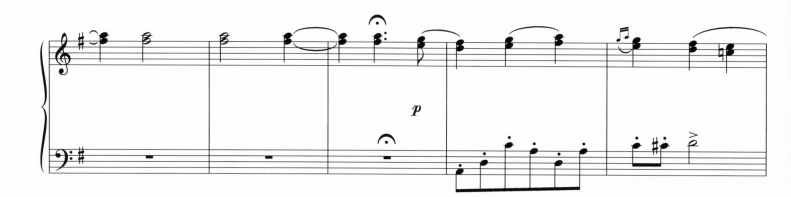

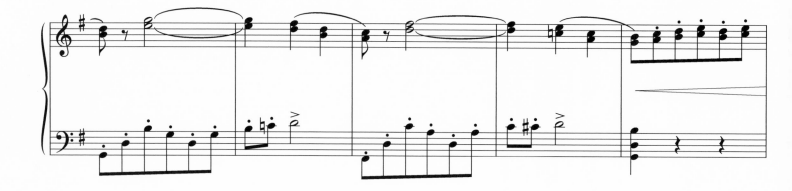

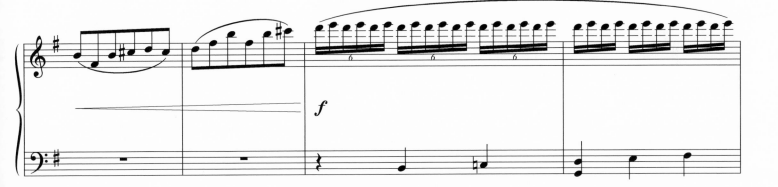

marcato

Serenade in C
Fourth Movement Excerpt
("Russian Theme")

Pyotr Il'yich Tchaikovsky
1840-1893
Op. 48
originally for strings

Allegro con spirito (♩ = 144)

Tempo I

ff marcatissimo

stringendo

Allegro con spirito

Più mosso

sempre **fff**

Serenade in C
Third Movement Excerpt
("Elegy")

Pyotr Il'yich Tchaikovsky
1840-1893
Op. 48
originally for strings

Larghetto elegiaco (♩ = 69)

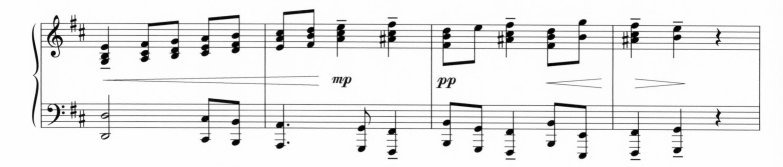

Sleeping Beauty Waltz
from the ballet THE SLEEPING BEAUTY

Pyotr Il'yich Tchaikovsky
1840-1893
Op. 66
originally for orchestra

Tempo di Valse

(Valse Lente)

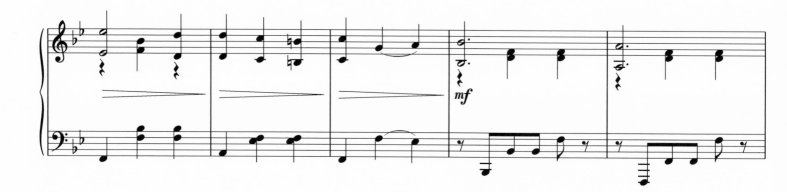

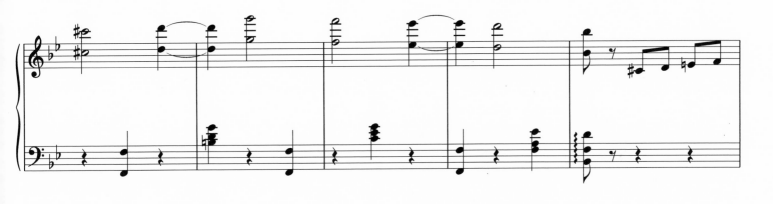

Hungarian Dance
("The Czars")
from the ballet SWAN LAKE

Pyotr Il'yich Tchaikovsky
1840-1893
originally for orchestra

Moderato assai

Allegro moderato

173

Waltz
from the ballet SWAN LAKE

Pyotr Il'yich Tchaikovsky
1840-1893
originally for orchestra

Tempo di Valse

Symphony No. 3 in D Minor
"Polish"
Third Movement Excerpt

Pyotr Il'yich Tchaikovsky
1840-1893
Op. 29
originally for orchestra

Andante elegiaco

Symphony No. 3 in D Minor
"Polish"
First Movement Excerpt

Pyotr Il'yich Tchaikovsky
1840-1893
Op. 29
originally for orchestra

Moderato assai (Tempo di marcia funebre)

pp   *poco stringendo*

Poco più mosso

p

dim.

185

Allegro brillante

Symphony No. 5 in E Minor

Third Movement Excerpt ("Waltz")

Pyotr Il'yich Tchaikovsky
1840-1893
Op. 64
originally for orchestra

Allegro moderato

Symphony No. 4 in F Minor
Second Movement Excerpt

Pyotr Il'yich Tchaikovsky
1840-1893
Op. 36
originally for orchestra

Andantino in modo di canzona

p semplice
ma grazioso

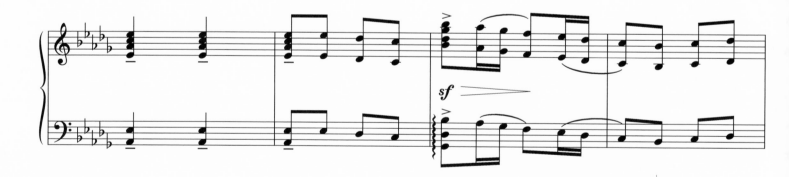

Symphony No. 6 in B Minor

"Pathétique"
First Movement Excerpt

Pyotr Il'yich Tchaikovsky
1840-1893
Op. 74
originally for orchestra

veneramente, molto cantabile con espressione

Adagio mosso

Andante mosso

Theme and Variation No. 3
from VARIATIONS ON A ROCOCO THEME
Excerpt

Pyotr Il'yich Tchaikovsky
1840-1893
Op. 33
originally for violoncello and orchestra

Moderato assai, quasi andante

THEME
Moderato semplice

VARIATION III
Andante sostenuto

Violin Concerto in D Major

Second Movement Excerpt, "Canzonetta"

Pyotr Il'yich Tchaikovsky
1840-1893
Op. 35
originally for violin and orchestra

Andante

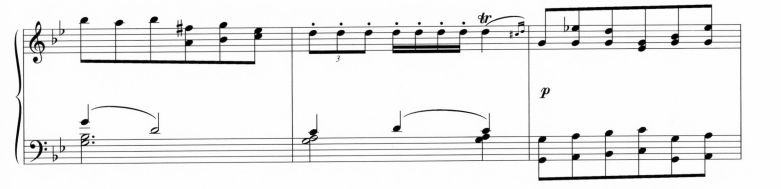

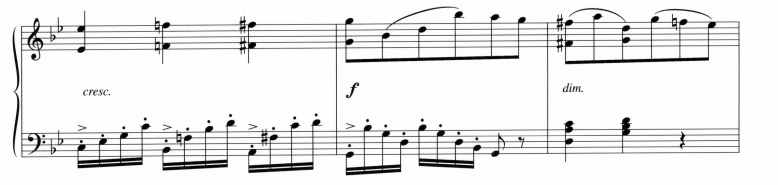

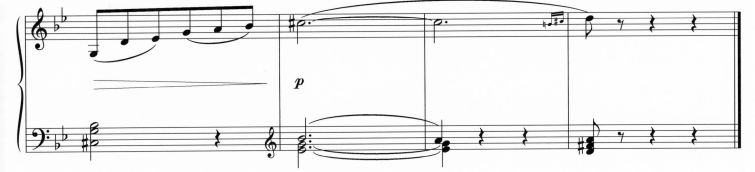

Violin Concerto in D Major

First Movement Excerpt

Pyotr Il'yich Tchaikovsky
1840-1893
Op. 35
originally for violin and orchestra

Waltz
from ALBUM FOR THE YOUNG

Pyotr Il'yich Tchaikovsky
1840–1893
Op. 39, No. 8

Vivace